With L To You

Penny Wyatt-Gold

Photography
Stephen & Penny Wyatt-Gold

Published by Reflex Books
(New Century Shows Ltd)

Printed and bound in the UK by Cloc Ltd. London

Author's website www.pennywyattgold.com

REFLEX BOOKS

www.reflexbooks.co.uk
reflexbooksales@gmail.com

This is your free music download

A special compilation of relaxing and inspiring
music to accompany my book.

One hour of gentle sounds to read by and enjoy.

Just go to
www.reflexbooks.co.uk/download.html
and click on the album cover

Thank you to Stephen

who always believes
that I can do more than
I think I can

I've believed him
and I have

Life is a series of bridges
Each one representing a new challenge
Some take a long time to cross and
Some are crossed with ease

Every bridge you cross
Takes you to a new destination
And every challenge you complete
Gives you a renewed sense of fulfilment

Embrace each bridge as a stepping stone
Leading to
A deeper understanding of yourself
And all that you are capable of

How would we learn and grow
if there were no more bridges left to cross?

I saw a bridge in the distance
It drew me nearer
I didn't know if it was real
Or a mirage in my head
As I got nearer it sparkled with light
I knew I had to step onto it
As I took the first step
The drawbridge lifted behind me
I knew I was on my way
And now there was no turning back

STEP ONTO THE BRIDGE
OF
NEW BEGINNINGS

Your life can be a magical experience

when you realise that you are its creator

Dreams come true
as long as you believe in them

Become one with your dreams

Believe
you can
and
you will

Your belief
in something
gives it
the power
to come true

When you truly believe in something

you infuse
every thought

and
live every moment

with the idea
of it being true

and so

it becomes
your reality

You are
who you believe yourself to be

Imagine your life as you want it to be
and you've begun to create it

The pictures in your mind
will create the reality in your life

Imagine
a magical bridge waiting to transport you
to all that you wish for

Life will re-arrange itself
around your inner feelings of what is
so as you journey across this bridge
have the feeling that your wishes
are already coming true

Allow yourself to be guided onwards
knowing that each encounter
is a stepping stone
to the fulfilment of your dreams

What you impress on your mind
is expressed in your life

Expect the best
and it will happen

When you expect something to come true
you are allowing it into your experience

Expectancy
creates a magnetism
which draws what you expect
into your life

so

always
expect the best

Doubts and fears

push your dreams away

Treat each doubt and each fear
as a little child trying to feed on your attention

Surround each one with love and watch it fade away

When
you let go
of the past
the future
sails
into view

Dwelling on the past
wastes time and energy
and
prevents you
from moving forward

Release the past
acknowledge where you are now
and the future
will appear on the horizon

What can you do today that will make a difference
to tomorrow?

Open up to the power within you

POSITIVE
THOUGHTS
BUILD BRIDGES

Think positively about life
and life becomes a positive experience

Decide that today
is going to be
a good day
and
it will be

A negative thought
is a precious moment wasted

Negative thoughts create more negativity

Negativity
eats up your energy
and weakens
your immune system

Positivity renews it

Thinking positively
takes practice

The best time
to start practicing
is now

A loving thought is a positive thought

What you are thinking now
will make a difference to the rest of your day

A positive thought has the power
to clear the way to positive outcomes

Gratitude creates a bridge
which draws more
of what you're thankful for
into your life

A grateful thought is a positive thought

The world
around you
is a
reflection
of
your
inner
thoughts

Life is
continually mirroring
your thoughts
about it

Your inner thoughts
create your outer reality

Before reacting negatively
PAUSE
and find a way to react positively

You make something a reality
by the way you think about it

A thought creates a bridge
which connects you to your desire

A negative thought weakens the bridge

A positive thought strengthens it

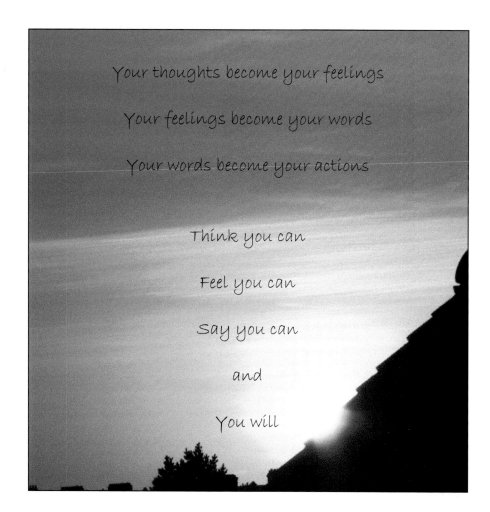

Your thoughts become your feelings

Your feelings become your words

Your words become your actions

Think you can

Feel you can

Say you can

and

You will

BE LED
BY
YOUR FEELINGS

Your feelings are your friends

They let you know
if you're heading in the right direction

Positive thoughts
create good feelings

Good feelings let you know
that everything is working perfectly

Feeling sad attracts more sadness

Feeling happy attracts more happiness

Your emotions
are the direct result
of your thoughts

Change your thoughts
and you change
how you feel

When the leaves begin to turn
you might think ...

Autumn will soon be followed by
the cold dark nights of winter
and it will seem an age before
spring is on its way

However,
life changes
when we change how we feel about it
so could it be that ...

The changing colours of autumn will
soon be followed by the cosy nights of winter
which tell us that
the new growth of spring
is just around the corner

Different thoughts
create different emotions

It's not what you do
but the feeling that you put in to what you do …

that makes a difference

The pleasure received
when something is done
with the feelings of
love, joy and happiness
far outweighs
the despondency felt
when something is done
with a feeling of negativity

Find enjoyment in whatever you do
and the outcome will be
more satisfactory

Listen to the wisdom of your heart

When you listen to your heart
you will find the answer that you've been searching for

Listen to your heart
even if
you don't understand
where it is leading you

The wisdom of your heart
is expressed by your feelings

When you feel something is right
you know
that you've been given the answer

The antidote to any pain
is to find something to feel good about

There is always something to love
There is always someone to love
You are always being loved

Fill your heart with love

Pain cannot feed on love

Tomorrow will reflect your feelings about today

Make tomorrow as beautiful as it can be

When you feel as if
you're pushing against the tide
turn round and flow with it

If it feels good do it

If it doesn't
move on to something else

CROSS THE BRIDGE
TO
SUCCESS

It's not a bad day -
it's just a different experience

Without the little dips in life
we wouldn't appreciate the highs

Life
is full of
ups and downs

and
the downs
always show us
a better way
back up

The secret of success

is to find the gift at the heart of any problem

Every problem

creates an opportunity

to discover

something new

The more you take advantage
of these opportunities
the more successful you will be

The more you talk about a problem the bigger it gets

The more you talk about a solution the nearer it appears

Mistakes
are only avoided
if you don't
try anything
new

Take the plunge

Don't tread water
when you have
the opportunity
to swim

So you think yesterday was a bad day?

What did you learn
from yesterday
that can make a difference
to today?

Everything
and everyone
has something
to teach us

Discover the gem
waiting to be found
within
every encounter

Perhaps yesterday
was a good day
in disguise

If you fail but learn from your mistake
you've had a success

Geniuses always learn from their mistakes

That's how they become a genius

Whatever you do
creates a result

What seems
a failure today
could turn out to be
a blessing tomorrow

Mistakes happen for a reason

Mistakes are learning experiences

Sometimes the problem is ...

that you think there's a problem

Imagining
all that could possibly go wrong
produces worry and fear

When your fearful thought becomes a belief
you've created a magnetic bridge
which draws that belief into your life

Walk away from fear
and
surround yourself with the powers of love and trust

Infuse yourself with the feeling
that your solution has been found

Solutions come to those who believe in them

Yesterday it rained and you were fed up

Today you are marvelling
at how the rain brought the flowers out

Life works
but your interpretation of it may need some adjusting

If you get yourself into a hole climb back out

If there's
a way
in
there's
a way
out

A butterfly
emerges from a cocoon
stronger and more beautiful
than it was before

KEEP MOVING
FORWARDS

Until you have a goal
life is powerless
to lead you in a forward direction

The first step in getting anywhere is
knowing where you want to go

When you know where you're heading
life will provide the transport

Maintain your belief
and allow the Universe
to show you how inventive it can be

Stay in the middle of the road
and you'll get nowhere

Make a decision
and you'll get somewhere

Intention is a powerful energy

Decide what you want

intend to get it

and a path will appear to take you there

You are now
at the starting point of your journey to
where you intend to be

In this moment you are creating your future

Feel excited about what lies ahead

If you reach a dead end
it's time to take a new direction

Life is full of twists and turns

To keep moving forward
you often have to adapt along the way

You can always go one step further
than you think you can

Until you try
you won't know how far you can go

If you play it safe
today
you'll get no further
than you did yesterday

When you move out of your comfort zone
you discover talents
you never knew you had

The first step is the hardest

Take that
first step
and

the next
will start to
unfold

Then everything
falls into place

The closer you get to uncharted territory
the more you realise that you can conquer it

When you take a step into the unknown
what seems strange at first
soon becomes familiar

The unknown
has the potential to be surprisingly good

There is always a way

Do you follow the same path every day
even though something is telling you
to try a different one?

Take one step
in a different direction
and you open up an avenue of opportunities

Opportunities to reach our goals
are always being presented to us

There is a reason behind every coincidence

Nothing is random

Don't walk through life blindfolded

Be aware of any opportunity being offered to you

It just might be the way

If you're not yet where you want to be
the journey isn't over

You will reach your destination
when you have absorbed all that there is to learn
along the way

How will you know when you get there?

When you start planning
the next journey

Life is a field of pure potentiality
waiting to be discovered

The enjoyment of life
comes from the participation in it

Enjoy taking part in the adventure

LIFE'S RICHES ARE
WAITING
TO BE DISCOVERED

If you are forever chasing deadlines
the magic of life can pass you by

Slow down
and connect with where you are

You'll notice things you didn't know were there

When you appreciate what you have
life is ready and willing
to give you more

We live in the energy that surrounds us

This isn't someone else's world

This energy is your world

Make friends with it
love it
respect it
and
it will work miracles for you

Negativity pollutes your world

Your world
wants to be loved
and
when it is
all will be well

Saturate the energy
around you with positivity and love

When you treat each day as a gift
each day becomes very special

Life is magical when you embrace its magnificence

Every day you are being offered new ways
to experience the gifts of life

When you are focused on
complaints, negativity and worries of 'what if'
these beautiful gifts
can't find a way through to you
and so they go away
hoping to be accepted another day

Connect with each gift
and be open to receiving all that it can offer you

Today is very special because
yesterday is a memory and tomorrow is yet to come

This moment
is part of
this very special day

Make it count

When you start taking life for granted

you stop seeing
how amazing
it is

When you stop taking life for granted
you see it in a different light

Everything you need is here
waiting for you to acknowledge it

Feel a river of peace flowing through you today

Peace within creates peace without

Listen to the silence

It's where questions are answered

If you're
feeling stressed

breathe

It's simple
and it's free

Calm people
breathe
calmly

Moments with friends are moments to be treasured

Make time for the important things in life

True friends always appear just when you need them

What you focus on grows

Focus on the miracle of life
and life becomes more of a miracle

Miracles happen every day ...

if you believe in them

Time spent in nature is re-energising

Everyone needs time
to reflect on how truly beautiful life is

Be kind to yourself

A
BRIDGE OF LOVE
IS BECKONING
YOU

You might not see love
but you can feel how its presence
makes a difference

Love is the energy
that binds us

Without love
our world would
fall apart

As you sail through life
send out ripples of love

Ripples of love
negate waves of turbulence

Love is the ingredient that makes things happen

What you look at with love grows in value

Why wait till tomorrow to tell
someone you love them?

We all want to be loved

It's our life force

Unlock the door to your heart
to release the love that is waiting there

When you withhold love
you inhibit your true flow

Love is the key
that unlocks a closed heart

Be
rich in love

If there are muddy waters between you and another

build a bridge of love
to cover the expanse between you

Giving love
opens
the doorway
to
receiving
love

Whatever the problem the answer is always love

Love changes everything

When you're filled with love
nothing can hurt you

Love dissolves all negativity

You live with yourself all the time

It's much nicer to live with someone you love

and

when you love yourself you become more loveable

Love is all around you

Bathe in its warmth

Bathe in its healing properties

Bathe in its joy that you've discovered it

When something is broken
mend it
and make it stronger than it was before

Anything built on a foundation of love
lasts forever

Everything and everyone has a heart

Touch the heart of what you desire with your heart
and
let love bring you together

You live in a sea of love

The tide might recede
but it never fails to return

Allow yourself to be different
because everyone else is

We are all unique and that's
what makes us so special

Let's
embrace our differences
and
appreciate our similarities

Be
true
to yourself

If you follow someone else
make sure they're going in your direction

Someone else's way
may not be your way

Many routes
reach the same destination

Find the one
that works for you

When you get a good idea
do more than just whisper about it

Be someone who makes things happen

Life's too short to remain in the shadows

Be a magnificent person in a magnificent world

If you pull back from life
you reduce your capacity to experience
all that it has to offer

Life wants your presence to be felt

We are all an important cog in the big wheel of life

Without you the world would be a different place

You make a difference

A SMILE
WILL HELP YOU
ON YOUR WAY

You are a vehicle for pure joy

Resist
that joy
and
the vehicle
breaks down

Allow the joy of life
to radiate from every part of your being
and your journey will be a fulfilling one

Smile

and problems fly away

It takes a lot of energy to remain sad

Smile and you change how you feel

When you change how you feel
life changes around you

Smiling is a universal language
which makes the world a better and more unified place

Smiling
triggers
a
feeling
of
happiness

A smile
creates
a ray of
sunshine

Have you smiled yet today?

Happiness is infectious

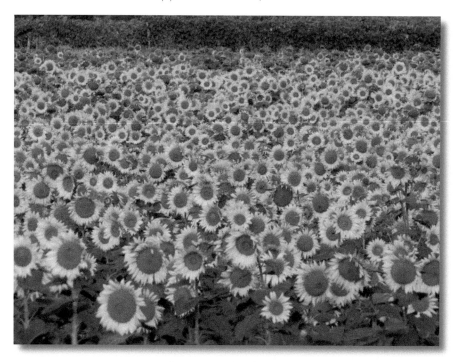

When you're happy
those around you are happy

Choose to be happy today

Happiness
is your natural state of being

Happiness enhances your health

Pressure
inhibits your ability to be happy

Having fun releases it

Put a measure of fun
into everything that you do

because

life is meant to be fun
and
you are meant to be happy

Add some sparkle into someone else's life ...

and you'll light up your own life too

Life
without sparkle
is like
champagne
without fizz

Happiness creates a feeling
of enthusiasm and optimism

You always achieve your best when you are happy

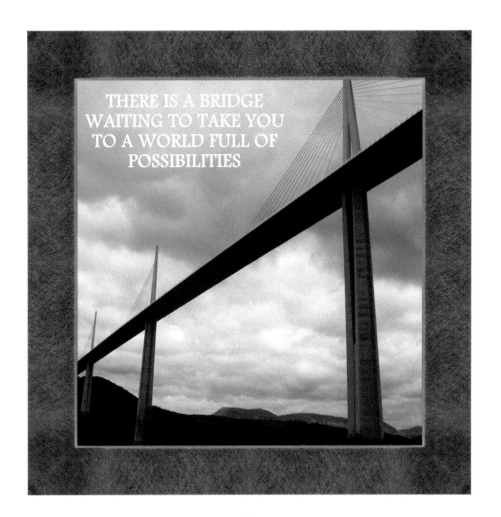

THERE IS A BRIDGE
WAITING TO TAKE YOU
TO A WORLD FULL OF
POSSIBILITIES

Never give up

What at first seems difficult
becomes easier with practice

A flower doesn't give up

It keeps on growing until it reaches the light
and then it blossoms into its full glory

Why stop
before you reach your full potential?

A tree has strong roots
and is always branching out in new directions

A sense of adventure
and a love of life
present opportunities
that you never knew existed

Stand tall, reach out
and embrace
all that life can offer

A bridge indicates a way across

When you meet someone halfway
a new bridge is formed

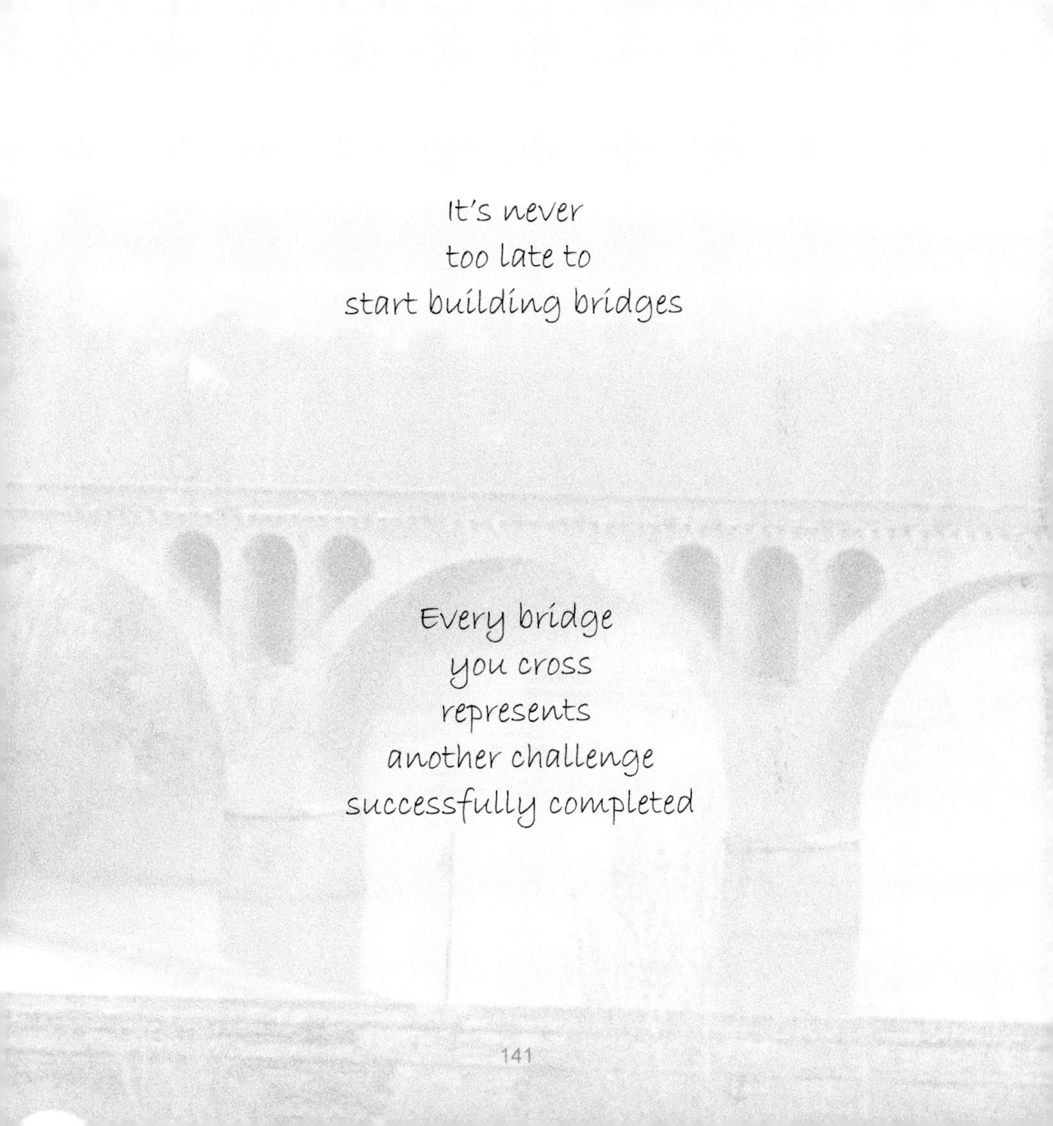

It's never
too late to
start building bridges

Every bridge
you cross
represents
another challenge
successfully completed

Stretch your mind to believe that anything is possible

Until you imagine it
it can't come true

A successful person never gives up

You only need to see a glimmer of light
to know that you're almost there

Narrow mindedness
makes your world smaller and less colourful

When you broaden your horizons
life becomes full of possibilities

Nothing is impossible to someone
with an open mind

Until you open the door
you don't know what's on the other side

What if all that you desire
is queuing up to enter into your life
but the door is closed?

The path you've just taken
has brought you to this door

Why did you follow the path
if you're reluctant to
complete the journey?

Release your fear, say yes to life
and open the door

Life is an ocean of possibilities
but catch them before they swim away

If life's moving forward
go with it

Don't put the brakes on

If you stand still
you might get left behind

The only way to get to the top
is to keep aiming higher

There is no limit to what you can achieve
unless the limit is placed there by you

You can
do it

High
expectations
lift you
higher

Life is meant to be easy
It's us who make it difficult

Belief in anything being possible
rather than impossible
makes it so

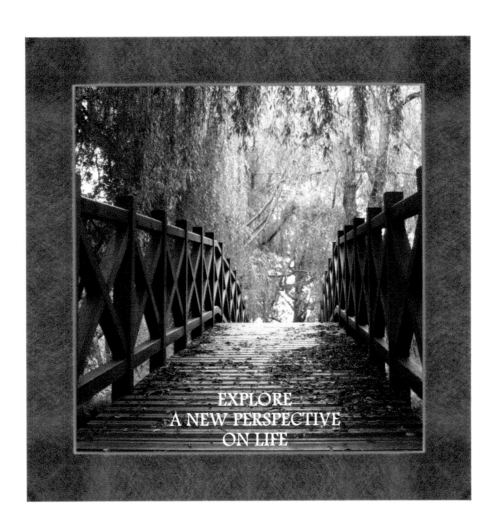

EXPLORE
A NEW PERSPECTIVE
ON LIFE

When everything starts to look the same
it's time for a new adventure

Change one thing in your life
and life changes around you

Different actions produce different results

Change your routine and life renews itself

Do the same thing in the same way every day
and nothing will change

Change your outlook on life

Forever looking at the same thing in the same way
means coming up with
the same conclusion

Saying you can't uses up a lot of energy
and closes doors

Put that energy into working out how you can
and you'll discover that
a closed door can always be opened

Be flexible

Too often one has a preconceived idea
of how things should be

The same situation can always be seen
from a different perspective

Not everyone
will see things
the same way that you do

When you look at things
from a different point of view
life takes on a new meaning

Feel safe enough
to be flexible

If life isn't flowing
what have you put in its way?

Resistance to anything
creates a barrier

The more you resist
the bigger the barrier

The bigger the barrier
the harder it is to find a way round it

Let go and let life flow

You will always flow in the right direction
when you allow life to lead you

Water never questions where it's going

It trusts
the pathway ahead

When it encounters
an obstacle
it flows around it

It doesn't waste time
remonstrating

Treat any obstacle as a gift
that helps you find a better way

Life has a natural rhythm to it

When you push against that rhythm
you become stressed and irritable

When you flow with it
life works perfectly

AS YOU CONTINUE
YOUR JOURNEY
REMEMBER …

Turn on the light and the darkness disappears

Let your own light shine

We all have an inner light shining bright
It helps light up our way
A negative thought dims that light
And brings a cloud to every day
Fill each day with love and laughter
And watch the negativity float away
Then once more you are that shining light
That conquers whatever comes your way

When the time is right
a new bridge will appear

When it does
accept the invitation and step onto it

Once on the bridge
you have a choice

Walk towards your dreams
or
turn back
and leave it for another day

but

if not today
when?

Doubt
is a lack of belief

Trust
creates the energy to carry you forward

Look at the
bigger picture

Every piece of the jigsaw of life
falls perfectly into place
when you allow it to

Behind every cloud there exists a ray of sunshine

Some of us only see the clouds

Some of us always look for the ray of sunshine

Look for the best in
everything
and
everyone
and
you will be
rewarded with
the best
that life can offer

The horizon is always bright
once the clouds begin to clear

Nothing
is as bad as it might seem

because clouds

never stay in the same place
for very long

The tide always turns

Ride any storm
knowing that calm waters
lie ahead

When you look at where you've been
you can see how far you've come

Life is a never ending journey

Thank where you've been
for revealing the pathway
to where you're going

Things might not turn out exactly
as you want

They often turn out better

I saw a bridge in the distance
It drew me nearer
I didn't know if it was real
Or a mirage in my head
As I got nearer it sparkled with light
I knew I had to step onto it
As I took the first step
The drawbridge lifted behind me
I knew I was on my way
And now there was no turning back

Thank you
to all those who love me
I love you too
and you make my world
a brighter place

Penny Wyatt-Gold

Penny Wyatt-Gold has been a highly experienced reflexologist and life coach in the UK and France for the past twenty years. In that time she also produced a number of fast-selling inspirational booklets which included relaxation music written by her husband Stephen. This book is the issue of years of experience in positive thinking for a better lifestyle.

Penny originally trained as an actress and dancer and went on to appear in many UK musical theatre productions followed by a successful career as a director and choreographer.

www.pennywyattgold.com

Dip into my book and relax to more music
by
Stephen Wyatt-Gold

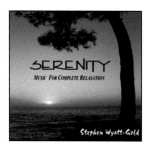

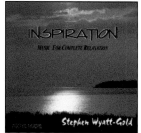

All albums are available from
Apple Music, **Spotify**, **Amazon**, **Deezer**,
YouTube Music *and all other music sites*

REFLEX BOOKS

www.reflexbooks.co.uk

reflexbooksales@gmail.com